Introduction to...

ITZME

A new refreshing outlook on healthy living.

It Takes Zeal Motivation & Energy

Vol. I

Contents

Acknowledgments   5

     INTRODUCTION   7

The Mind & Body

The Brain.. 9

The Heart.. 17

The Abdomen... 23

Muscles... 33

Tendons +Ligaments............................... 39

Joints... 45

Bones.. 51

    AFTERWORD   ***59***

Dear Reader,

Giving all honor and glory to the Heavenly Father of Life this book was written to both inform and inspire God's children of all ages and ethnicity. I thank you for purchasing this book and I hope once you've completed it you walk away wiser with a refreshed since of clarity. This book contains material that has been researched, experimented and experienced.

I personally believe the best attribution this book offers is its way of delivering a broad message that narrates to each reader or listener individually. This was done by first understanding every person is unique and so is each day. Two or more people sitting or standing next to each other may see the same image but they will see that image from different angles. Just imagine this same scenario with the same two people only this time they're facing each other from separate ends of a table. As they both experience life in the same environment the information received through their eyes will be opposite. People do however share a lot of the same emotions, pressures,feelings, desires, goals and even similar ideas from different angles as well. In a race to the finish line only one racer experiences 1st place(unless by chance there is a draw). Life itself isn't so competitive but it does present tests and challenges. It actually shows favoritism to each of us allowing the opportunity to make the most of it.

Experiences in life as we all know, consists of success and failures ,ups and downs ,and ins & outs that effect our emotions in either a positive or negative way. Positive or negative energy in motion can effect us mentally and physically for better or for worst.

This book promotes mental and physical well being and encourages others to do the same. Love is the inspiration of life. It endures all emotion and manifests happiness. It is the answer to life's challenges and tests.

No matter where or who you are, you have the God given ability to Love. In loving yourself be sure to take care of your mind and body to really get the most out of life. Life suggests it is never too late while Love asks why would you wait.
    Sincerely ~ITZME.

INTRODUCTION

There are 7 basic principals to life and survival. These principals are believed to be encoded in our DNA and are the substance of the basic instincts of a human. They are; **Feeding, Working, Resting, Learning, Reproduction, Communication and Protection.** Established since the beginning of Man they are still to this day the most important factors in the order of life. With this being stated. How much more important is it for our bodies and minds to function properly in order to execute these means of survival for as long as we are physically alive? In the course of this presentation we will take you inside and out the body in hopes to refresh your inner memory and raise related awareness. We'll also provide information on healthier living, finding inner peace, and achieving goals. All in all nothing is done without ability so we encourage you to answer the questions only you can answer. **Are you able to rise to a challenge? Are you willing to equip yourself with things necessary to practice and get back up when you fall?** Confidence and doubt come from within as a result of experiences and a persons ability to believe. Before we make final conclusions, lets take a look inside the body and get a better understanding of the mind.

The Brain...

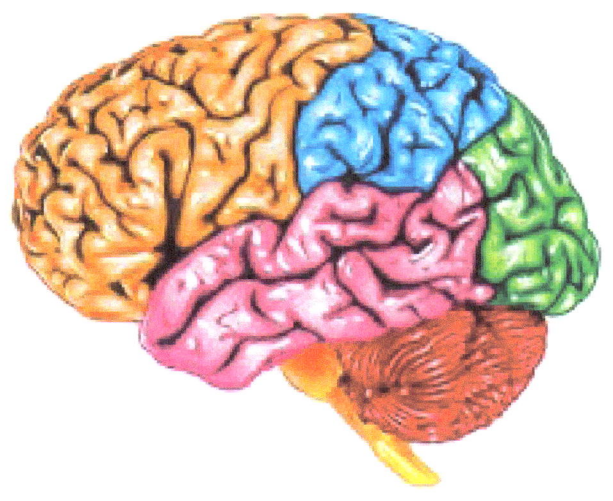

Brain

The brain located inside the scull functions as the center of nervous activity. It is also where sensation and intellect are manifested. Consuming up to 25% of the bodies converted glucose and 25% percent of the oxygen we breathe this organ is so vital and precious that if a person is diagnosed as brain dead he/she is scientifically no longer alive. Aside from containing billions of neurons, being 78% water and only weighing 2% the weight of a person who weighs 150 lbs; the brain has a direct connection to the faculties of consciousness and thought. This element of a persons awareness of the world,experiences,and feelings make up what we call the Mind(which contrasts the mental process with physical action or reaction). The left region of the brain controls the right side of the body while the right controls the left.

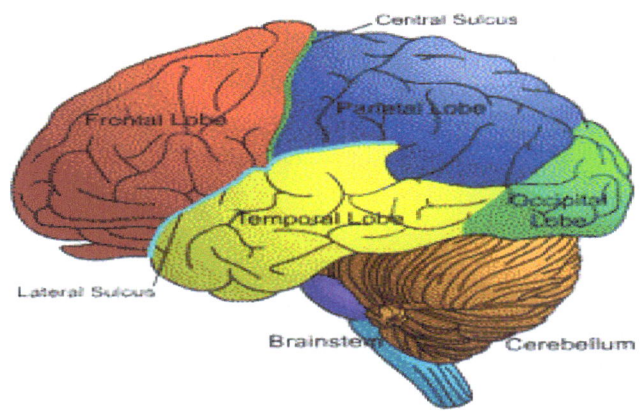

- The functions of the **frontal lobe** of the brain enables the ability to plan, reason, imagine, control motor skills and draw from memory.
- The **Temperal lobe** is responsible for the interpretation of sounds, languague and perception, storing long term memory, new memory and emotion.
- The **Parietal lobes** process information like sense of touch, relativity of numbers, pain and verbal memory.
- **Occipital lobes** located in the back of the brain process visual information.
- The **Cerebellum** along with use of other regions of the brain is most responsible for motor control such as; coordination, accuracy, equilibrium, motor learning and the posture of the body.
- The **Brain Stem** is a part of the Hind and Mid Brain that connects to the spinal cord and cerebellum. It controls the regulation of the central nervous system including; sleep regulation, consciousness while sleeping, eating, the heart rate, blood pressure, the motor and sensory in the face and neck, and also the connection of nerves from the main brain to the rest of the body.

All damage to the brain and mind would be due to any strain, damage, or hemorrhage in any of these regions

in the brain.
     Although the brain is seen as two hemispheres; the right and left side mirror each other with only microscopic differences in distribution. This varies from individual to individual.

Risks

Strokes -3rd leading cause of death in the U.S, Claiming 700,000 patients and 160,000 victims a year.
Heart Disease
Dementia
Epilepsy
Stress
+more

Requirements

Rest- Although the brain continues to function during sleep getting the proper rest keeps the brain refreshed. Researchers have found that getting proper rest actually enhances memory. Another way to give your hard working brain a break to rejuvenate energy is through meditation. Meditation is great for dealing with stress as well. Sleep deprivation can lead to stress,irritability,grumpiness, and an unexpected break down. A good nights sleep gives you the energy to make it through the next day as awake as an be.
Exercise- ever heard the phrase "use it or loose it" or how about "a mind is a terrible thing to waste"?
Well they're both true we just combine the two and say

"use it to your advantage." Your mind is a divine instrument that if trained enough in a positive direction can perform at exceeding levels that will allow you to explore all possibilities of life. Challenging the brain is like exercising a muscle except you may see quicker results. Information we gather as we learn are stored and help to ease through similar obstacles in the future.
Nutrition- The proper Minerals, Vitamins, Fruits, Vegetables, Nuts, Glucose,Oxygen,and fatty acids (fatty acids found in some fish) keep the brain healthy. Remember 15-20% of the blood in the body flows from the heart to the brain. Keeping the flow clear will eliminate chances of stroke or high blood pressure. Speaking of flow; Did you know the urge to drink fluids is actually a natural instinct that is regulated by negative feed back from the brain?

So as we learn about the brain, we learn more about the mind and begin to understand Life a little better. We find that Existence requires being awake,being Alive requires breathing, and maintaining the continuance of being requires using your mind. This Brain of ours helps us facilitate actions needed to execute tasks and enhance our lives. It takes a healthy mind to make this possible so it is beneficial for us to soul search from within to discover some of the answers needed to live a quality life. **What things or people do you value most? What is your purpose or aspiration in life? Who's in charge of you getting where you want to be? What steps need to be taken? Whats standing in your way?**

Lets try applying the brains function to the way we live. Thinking before acting and establishing the use of things connected allow us to facilitate our lives. Goals require a plan. Plans aren't Ideas they are the necessary steps after ideas become goals. Good plans consider all possibilities and ensure completion even if they are forced to change. You are ultimately in control of the decisions you make. Giving up your control jeopardizes the success of your desires. Be the brains of your operation and remember... A plan in action is a dream coming true.
None of this supports the theory of right brain and left brain thinkers.

The Heart..

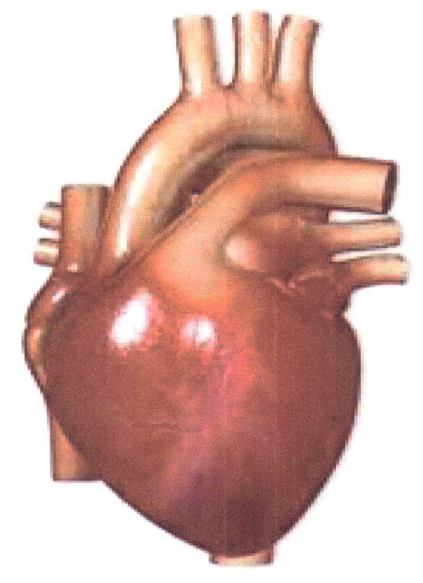

HEART

    The Heart; is located in the center of the chest slightly to the left between the lungs. The average heart is said to beat about 72 times a minute, 100,000 times a day, 35 million times a year, and about 2.58 billion times during a 66 year lifespan. This hollow muscular organ is the most vital part of the circulatory system and works twice as hard as the leg muscles during a sprint. With pulsating contractions the heart pumps blood throughout the blood vessels to various parts of the body. It is made up of a combination of cardiac muscle and connective tissue. The heart supplied by 5% of the bodies blood supply and has its own electrical impulse. This means it

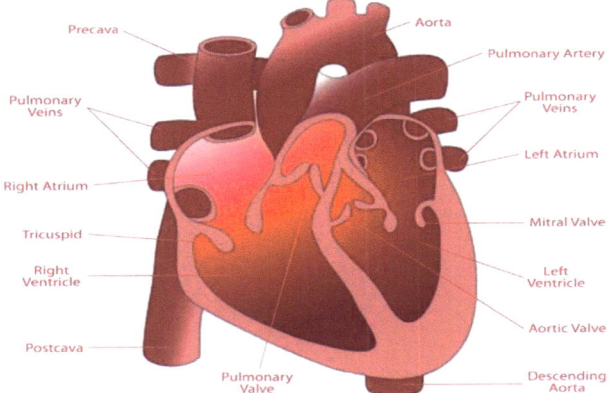

can continue to beat even when separated from the body as long as it has an adequate amount of oxygen. The blood pumped out by the heart carries important materials to designated places in the body (like the 20% of Glucose that goes to the brain) and removes wastes.

The right side of the Heart receives blood from the body then pumps it into the lungs enabling a process called diffusion allowing carbon dioxide to be exchanged for oxygen;while the left side receives blood from the Lungs and pumps it out to the body. There are four blood-filled areas of the heart called chambers; there are two on each side of the heart,two on the top and two on the bottom. The two on the top are atrium's called atria (they're responsible for taking in the blood from the lungs and the body). The two on the bottom are called ventricles (and they pump the blood out to the lungs and body) . Separating each side of the heart is the septum while four valves; The Tricuspid, Mitral Valve, Pulmonary Valve and Aortic Valve keep the blood flow in one direction, opening to let blood flow forward and closing to stop it from moving backwards.

RISKS
Stroke
Heart Attack
Heart failure
Heart disease
+more

Requirements

Exercise- does wonders for your heart. Vigorous exercising has proved to be one of the factors in people who live longer lives. This is a physical medicine and will prevent and even cure disease and different sicknesses. Laughter is a form of exercise as well, it feels great and your mind and body appreciates you for it. If you're in shape your insured.

Nutrition- Fruits and lots of vegetables are also good for a healthy heart. Nutrients supply the muscles with energy and are not foreign to the body, making the blood flow and digestion process smooth and productive. You really are in a lot of ways what you eat. If a person constantly eats unhealthy foods they are literally working against themselves and are at risk of heart attack, high blood pressure, ulcers,and clogged arteries. Don't eat a heart attack or ingest Diabetes its just not worth it friends.

It will also behoove you to quit or moderate smoking and drinking alcohol. That's if you want to stay alive.

As we learn more about the heart and get a closer look into the cycle of life. Without the heart to pump blood through the body we cannot live. This system of pumping , directing and circulating shows us how essential it is to keep this organ healthy and strong. If we apply this to life we see the importance of flow and direction. The less harmful and dangerous things we allow into our lives the easier life is. Stress is not only harmful to our bodies physically it also blocks happiness, peace and mental growth. Take financial stress for example. Financial stress comes from the feeling of inadequacy. Your needs become so apparent to you, your brain begins to work harder which increases the heart rate leaving you mentally/physically drained and a lot of times with a headache. This focus of your energy causes your body to react on the emotions when its primary function is to maintain physical existence. Placing too much focus on a circumstance clouds the mind from seeing the absolute best solution. Here's another example; Think about how bomb threat pranks would get us taken out of class when we were middle school students. We'd get a break, we'd laugh with our friends,and of course have some concern about the threat. We finally see it was a false alarm and are directed back to class, now having to refocus our energy. The teacher tells us to settle down and manages to get the class back in order.

      We can only change the things we have control over. If your only option is to acquire more money, focus your energy on doing so remembering to flow and not block the way. Sometimes we cant control our emotions but we can control our bodies. Try learning ways to manage the body under stress as if you were a teacher of a class after a bomb threat. Here are a few ways; **Take Slow Deep Breaths remembering breathing is living. Take a walk or jog. Meditate clearing your mind of all the pressures of life during this process.** As you do this, focus on the functioning of your body and mind taking place. You'll then find your self in a more relaxed place to get your class in order. **Explore your options. Never Give Up. Find Direction .And Flow.**

The Abdomen..

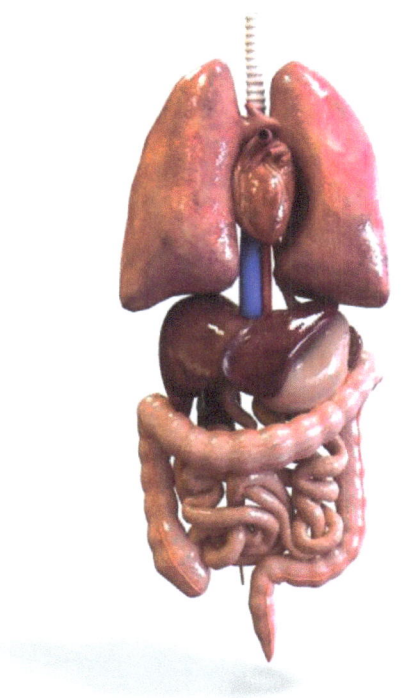

ABDOMEN

The Abdomen is located under the chest and above the pelvis. The abdominal cavity enclosed by abdominal muscles is where absorption and digestion occur. These muscles along with the back muscles primarily protect the organs inside the abdominal cavity, support the bodies posture and assists with breathing. The diaphragm separates the heart, lungs and ribs from the abdomen and contracts allowing air to enter the lungs. The Aorta(pink colored) is the largest artery in the body. Connected to the left ventricle of the heart it distributes oxygenated blood to all parts of the body. Shaped almost like a crowbar the aorta descends from the heart down into the abdomen then divides into two smaller arteries called the common iliac arteries. The Inferior Vena Cava (Blue colored) sits behind the abdominal cavity & carries deoxygenated blood(containing carbon dioxide) from the lower body into the right atrium of the heart. It also joins with the common iliac arteries. Let's take a look at some of the other organs

The **Kidneys** (bean shaped) remove waste products from the blood and regulates water fluid levels. 22% of the bodies blood supplies the kidneys through the renal artery. The blood is then passed through the kidneys nephrons and the access fluid/waste pass from the bloodstream through the ureter;then down to the bladder then out the bladder. The kidney helps the body to regulate temperature inside the abdomen, electrolyte concentration and blood pressure.

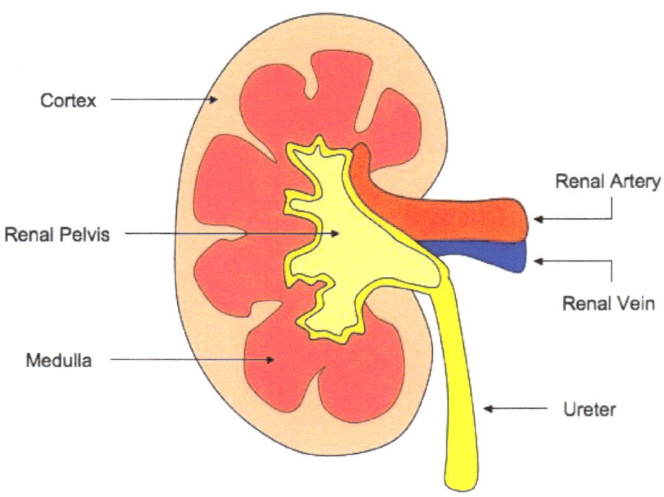

The cortex and the medulla of the adrenal glands synthesize and secrete hormones that helps the kidneys to preserve sodium & water.

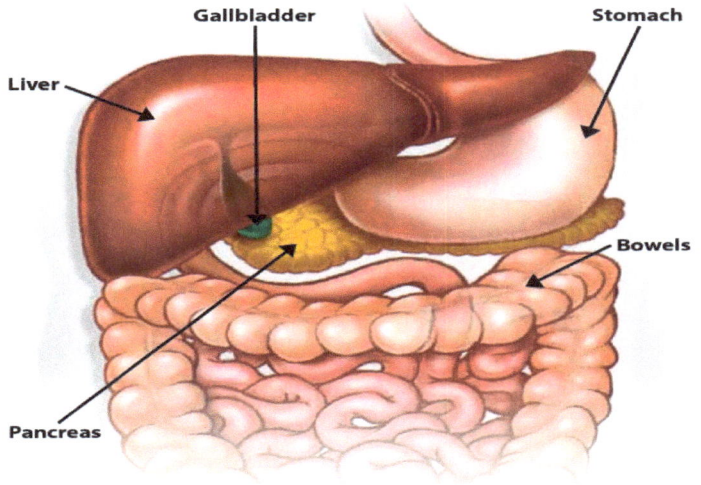

The **Gallbladder** is where bile is made by the liver (which helps breaks down fat)and stored before it is released into the small intestine. A human doesn't necessarily need this organ to live although its function is useful to a healthy body. The most common problem associated with this tiny pear shaped sac is called the gallstone; a small hard concretion of cholesterol, bile pigments, and lime salts, formed in the Gall bladder. Can be very painful.

The **Spleen** plays a major role in blood purification and in the immune system. If removed the liver would have to take a portion of its role in germ fighting and coordinating the immune system which may very well increase chances of an infection. The spleen produces a white pulp that produces and grows immune & blood cells; and a red pulp that is responsible for removing dead or old cells.

The **Liver** is the largest organ and gland in the body. Divided by two lobes the liver produces bile and plays a vital role in metabolism. The liver is also responsible for hormone production, decomposition/production of red blood cells &detoxification. The body doesn't survive in its absence and because of its wide variety of functions the liver is prone to many diseases. The most common would be cancer,cirrhosis, alcohol damage and hepatitis.

The **Pancreas** below the stomach is a digestive organ that helps the body with breaking down carbohydrates,proteins and the absorption of nutrients in the small intestine. It produces hormones like insulin & glucagon that help the body regulate the distribution of nutrients and glucose.

The **Stomach** is located between the esophagus and the small intestine. A part of the second phase of digestion the stomach stores food then breaks it down for digestion along with the help of a few digestive acids and muscles. The food is churned by muscle contractions and digested into chyme. When all the nutrients have been absorbed the remaining wastes passes to the rectum to be stored until its released from the body.

The **Small Intestine** about 21-23 feet long is where most of digestion occurs. The small intestine breaks down fats and proteins into fatty acids then absorbs the nutrients and minerals. Food takes about 4 hours to work its way through this tubular organ. Which is slightly longer in the female body.

The **Large Intestine** also called the colon is about five feet in length and is the last part of the digestive system. It absorbs water from left over indigestible foods then passes useless waste from the body. The large intestine contains over 700 species of bacteria that produce vitamins, gas and antibodies.

Risks
cancer
tumors
sickle cell
high blood pressure
low blood pressure
heart disease
kidney failure
diabetes
Gall Stones
Kidney Stones
+more

Requirements
Nutrition-Fruits and green and yellow vegetables are rich in nutrients that are needed for a healthy digestive system. Fiber found in foods like whole grains, apples, broccoli, carrots, spinach, beans and some cereals help not only with dieting, but also with digesting foods and even preventing cancer. Probiotic foods like yogurt, bananas, garlic and asparagus help the body to fight off sicknesses and are beneficial to the colons lining. Sunflower seeds, Dark chocolate, avocado and olives are just a few foods that contain minerals that prevent fat from accumulating around the abdomen. And we cant for get to drink Water, Water + Water.

Exercises- ab exercising helps to build muscle that protects the organs, assist in breathing and burns belly fat. Keeping active is beneficial in relieving the body of wastes and toxins. Keep sweating.

We now have a better understanding of how where and why food is processed and distributed into nutrients. The body runs on the fuel we consume and would eventually shut down if we ever cease to do so. Adding to the nutrients, minerals and probiotics the body produces increase productivity,energy and immunity. The relationships between the nervous system, respiratory system and digestive system are unbreakable. Applied to life outside the body, we see that nothing operates without a core and some relation to its surroundings. Taking in the necessities and disposing of the wastes makes room for the new & helps us to better organize our lives. Organization reduces stress and hassle. There's no need store anger and sadness inside let it out, remembering to separate the waste from the lesson learned first. Try releasing it verbally. This could be sitting down and talking something out with someone or calling out the negative for what it is. Weather your alone or expressing yourself to others be sure make it clear that it is the waste you no longer want to carry. This doesn't involve fighting or throwing verbal blows it is simply recognizing the harmful negativity and understanding the long-term effects it will have if it continues to dwell inside of you. Forgiveness will be the most important factor in this process because it is the only way to continue with a positive outcome. Taking the good with the bad doesn't require holding on to the bad.

The Muscles..

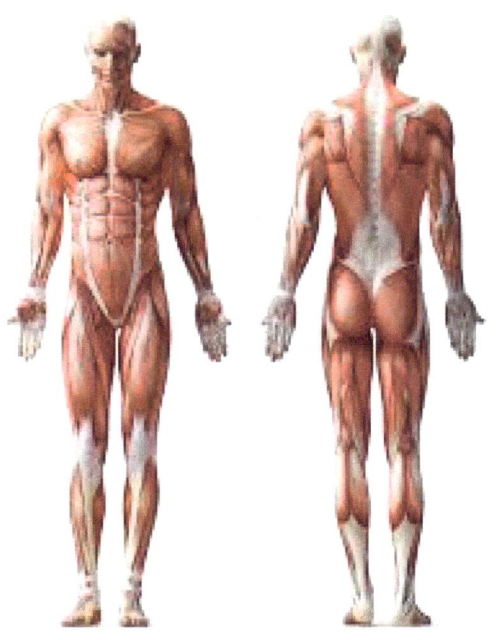

Muscles

There are 650 muscles and 187 joints in every human. Muscles are responsible for producing force and motion inside and outside the body. There are 3 types of muscles, the skeletal muscles that contract on command and the cardiac and smooth muscles that are classified as involuntarily. Skeletal muscles primarily maintain posture. They make up 42% of the average adult males body and 36% of the average adult female. Smooth muscles are found within the inner linings of many of the bodies organs and blood vessels and Cardiac muscles are found only in the heart. The Striated muscles which are

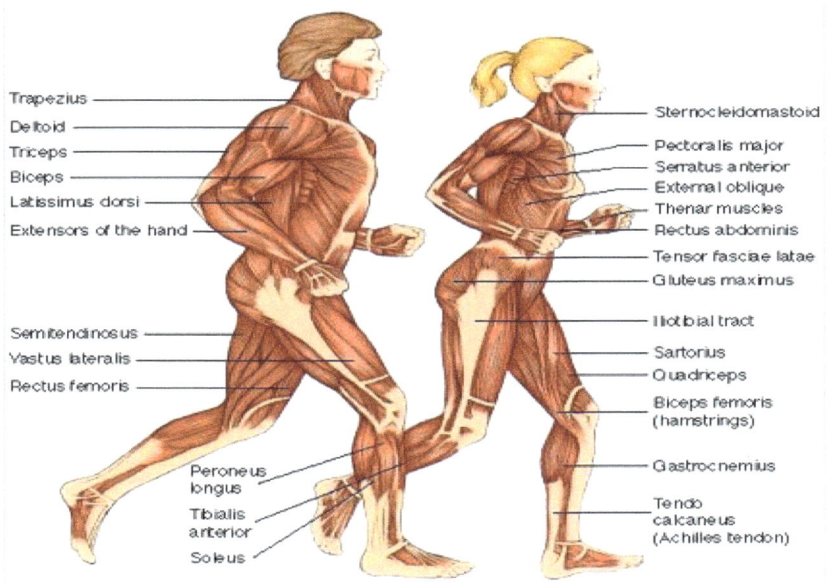

skeletal and cardiac muscles contract and relax in short

bursts while smooth muscles sustain contractions.

There are two types of muscles divided in Skeletal muscles . Type 1 (slow twitch fibers) carry oxygen by using fats, protein and carbohydrates as fuel allowing longer periods of contractions. Use of type one fibers would be long distance running and aerobic exercises. Type 2 (fast twitch fibers) usually used in sprinting or weight lifting cannot be sustained for longer periods of time. Fast twitch muscle fibers consume less oxygen, fats and protein, but produces larger amounts of lactic acid.

Risks
paralysis
stroke
Parkinson's disease
weakness
ruptures

Requirements

Nutrition- Much of the bodies energy consumption goes to the muscles. The muscle uses protein, glucose and carbohydrates as fuel. Foods like fish, shell fish(muscles), cereals, vegetables, fruit, soups and pastas are apart of a healthy muscle diet as well as Raw juices, Vitamin C, Vitamin E & water.
Exercise- exercising will improve motor skills, muscle and bone strength, and joint function. Slow twitch and Fast twitch exercises including swimming, bike riding,

and playing sports are good choices for maintaining healthy blood flow, strength, and endurance of the muscles.

Rest- Overworked muscles tear, tighten and involuntarily constrict during muscle fatigue resulting in a spasm or rupture . Getting physical therapy or massage will help relax the muscles and promote blood flow.

From lifting and running to pumping and smiling, muscles are a major factor in our lives. Muscles not only make us look more attractive, they also aid the body in every physical activity. The muscles in the face alone help us to communicate and show affection. Muscles consume lots of energy and enable the ability to physically get things done.

A healthy lifestyle will require much muscle use and will help you to be stronger and more productive. If we apply the muscles function to our lives we would first have to understand that all tasks aren't easily completed. There are circumstances and challenges in life that may require larger amounts of energy and force. This would cause you to use not only fuel for the body, but fuel for the mind as well.

Mental fuels like Motivation and Inspiration are 2 great sources of energy that can be used to help you push your way to completion. What gets you motivated? Who or what Inspires you?

Progression in life often seems to be an up hill journey and in order to reach our goals and aspirations we must commit to the climb. Every great achievement in the history of the world was fueled by great sources of motivation and/or Inspiration. It is very rewarding to achieve something from the muscle. Exercising self discipline helps you to gain the control to remain focused, inspired and motivated. Strength can also be manifested through the Courage to face challenges, the Zeal to learn, and Faith to remain confident. With stronger minds better decisions are made.

Tendons & Ligaments

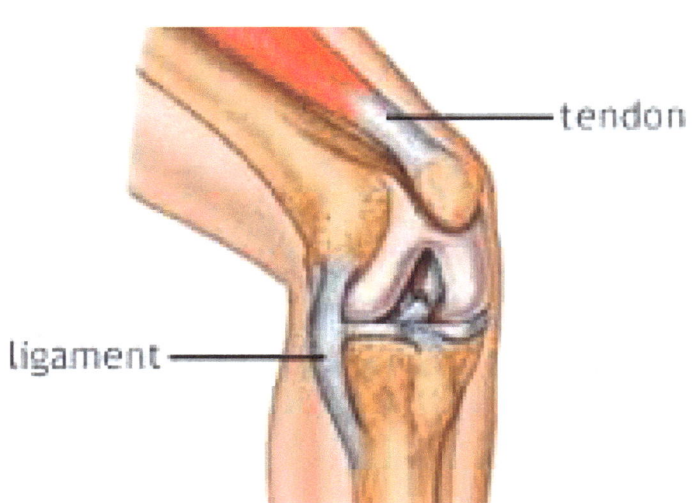

Tendons

Tendons bind muscle to bone. This tough & flexible fibrous tissue is made of collagen and aids the muscles in moving the bones. Tendons have different roles throughout the body and vary in length from person to person depending on muscle size. For example Bodybuilders generally have shorter tendons while swimmers and basketball players benefit from longer tendons. Tendons that extend are called extensor tendons and tendons that are involved in flexion are called Flexor tendons. Fingers and toes have extensor tendons on top and flexor tendons on the bottom. The strongest tendon in the body is the calcaneal tendon which is also called the Achilles tendon. Named after a Greek idol who's weakness was a injured eponymous tendon, the Achilles tendon connects the calf to the heel bone and is very prone

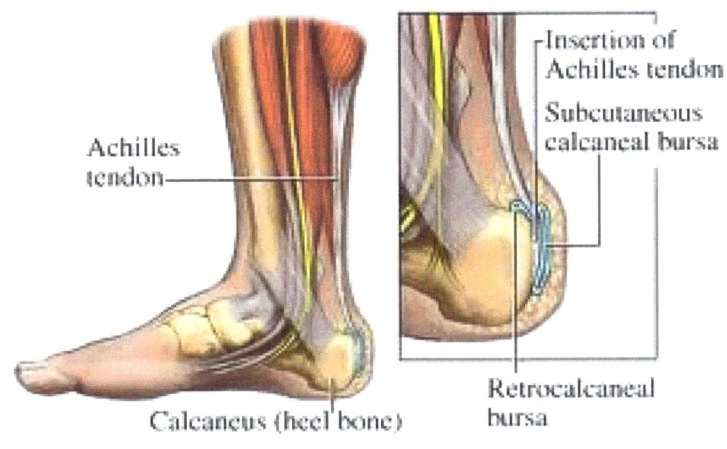

to injury.

A broken tendon is very painful and rehabilitation after intricate repair could take up to a year. Common injuries associated with the tendons are tendonitis and boutonniere deformity. Moderate stretching helps to keep the tendons flexible.

Ligaments

Ligaments are the fibrous connective tissue that connect bones to each other. Also made of collagen these stretchy viscoelastic tissues keep the range of the bones motion in control. Ligaments also protect organs, store energy and enable parts of the body to extend and flex. An overstretched ligament causes the joint to become weaker and less flexible. The most common injury associated with the ligament would be a sprain which typically happens when the ligament is stretched past normal capacity unexpectedly. Another common injury is damage done to

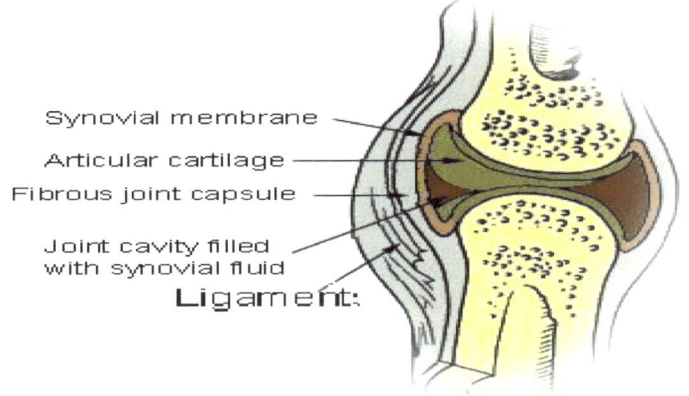

the Anterior Cruciate Ligament or (ACL),located behind the knee which occurs most often in highly intense sports and activities. A torn or ruptured ligament would definitely require surgery while less serious injuries require physical therapy.

Risks
Tear
Rupture
break

Requirements

Nutrition-.Ligaments and tendons are primarily made of proteins. Keeping proteins in your daily diet helps the body produce new collagen and elastic that make ligaments and tendons stronger in function. Ligaments and tendons contain calcium, so a healthy intake of calcium found in vitamin D will assist in healthy function. Vitamin C in fruits and vegetable also help produce collagen. Ligaments and tendon also contain Copper (in Nuts and Seeds) and Manganese (found in fish, bread and beans)
Exercise- exercises that help strengthen posture and everyday movements are essential in the sinews function. Walking , Squats as well as exercises for the shoulders, back and chess strengthen tendons,ligaments and muscles. Some lifting may be required but make sure you consult with a physician before heavy lifting.
Rest- if soreness or injury occur the best thing to do is relax them for a while. Icing,massaging and slowly graduating to rehabilitation will help them to heal properly and timely.

Joints

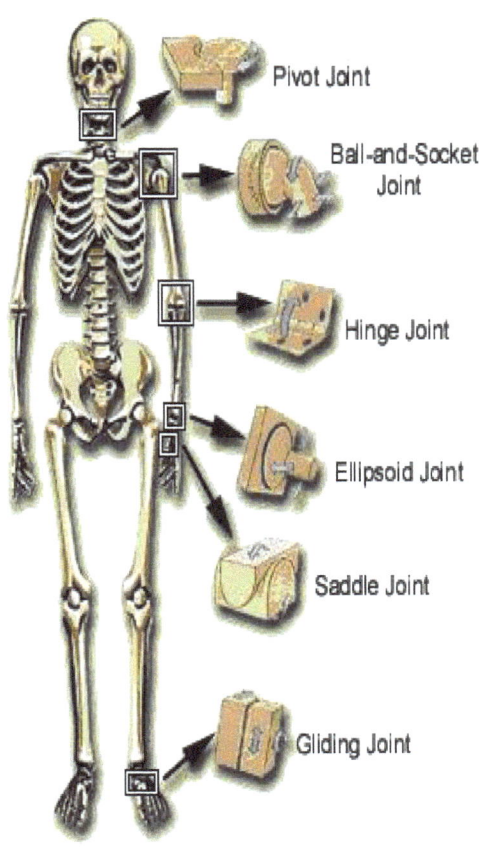

Joints

Joints are where bones join together allowing mechanical movement of the body. Joints are classified structurally or functionally. Joints that are structurally classified are determined by the way the bone is connected, and joints that are functionally classified are determined by the degree of movement between the connected bones, They can also be classified biomechanically or anatomically which depend on the number of bones involved.
  There are three Structural classifications that are named according to the tissue that connects the bones. They are: the fibrous joint which is joined by connective tissue containing collagen fibers, the cartilaginous joint joined by cartilage, and the synovial joint usually seen between the ligaments joined by bones that are not directly connected.
  The Functionally classified joints are: synarthrosis found in the skull permitting little or no mobility, amphiarthrosis mostly in cartilaginous joints permitting slight mobility, and diarthrosis joints
equivalent to the synovial joint allow free movement and can also be classified into six groups according to the movements they allow. These groups are arthrodia,articulation by reciprical reception,condyloid articulation, enarthrosis,ginglymus and rotaty diarthrosis.
  The Biomechanically classified joints are the simple joint; joints connecting two surfaces or bone

structures, the compound joint; joining 3 or more bone structures and the complex joint; or combination joint that joins 2 or more structures to an articular disc or meniscus.

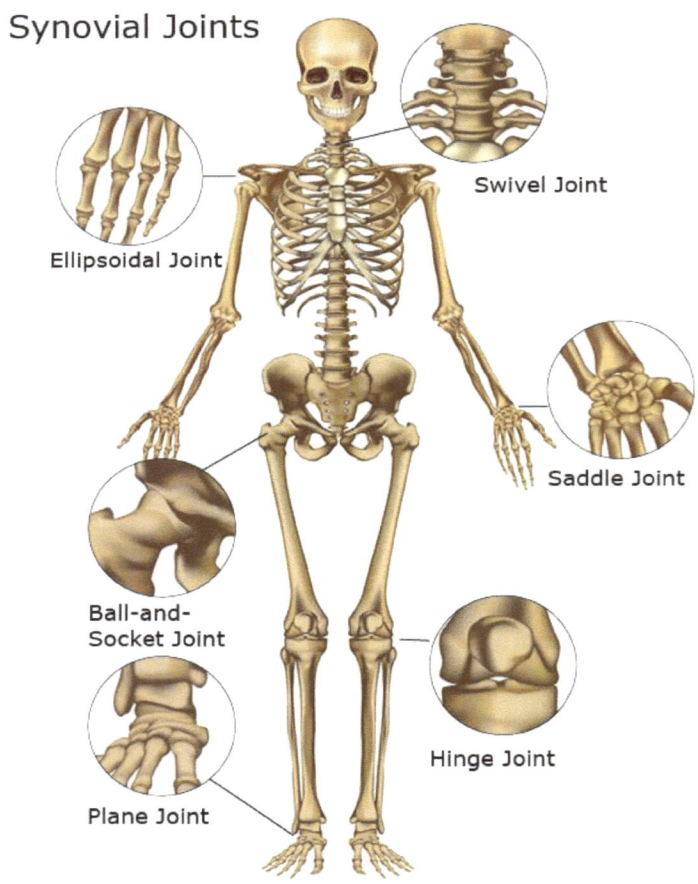

Risks
Arthritis
Gout
osteoarthritis
fibromyalgia
+more

Requirements

Nutrition- a few of the most beneficial nutrients to joints are amino acids, omega 3 fatty acids and vitamin D. Amino acids produce proteins and are found in foods like eggs , beans peanut butter, and even steak. Omega 3 fatty acids are usually found in fish oil or fish like salmon, mackerel & tuna. The vitamin D produced by sun exposure make for healthy bones and joints.
Exercise- Walking, swimming, light lifting, abdominal exercises and stretching all help promote healthy joint function. Your posture is very important in balancing the weight on your body. As pressure pressure weighs down on bones it would be helpful to maintain a healthy weight to prevent joint issues. A strong core and walking help us to stay erect in daily movement and even sitting.
Rest- as we age joints may stiffen or experience some pain. To prevent joint diseases it is essential to take pressure off the joints before they are overworked. If pain occurs you can ice them which will also reduce swelling.

Bones..

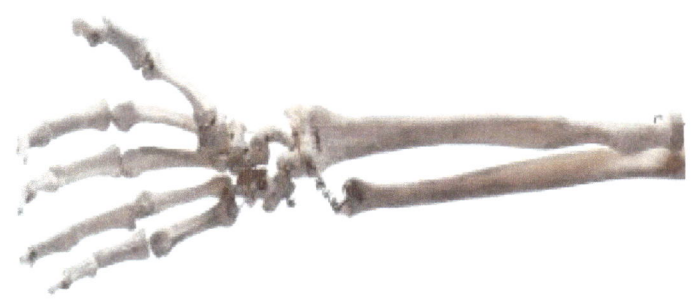

Bones

Bones come in a variety of shapes and sizes as we all know. Light in weight and surprisingly strong bones not only support and protect the organs of the body; bones also produce red and white blood cells and store minerals. There are 206 bones in the adult body. The bone is made of a combination of tissues which are marrow, cartilage, blood vessels, nerves, endosteum, periosteum, and osseous tissue. Compact bone tissue or dense bone makes up 80% of the bone mass of an adult and gives bones their solid white appearance. The tubercular bone accounts for the remaining 20% of bone mass and is composed of a network of rod and plate like elements that allow room for blood vessels and marrow. It also makes the overall organ lighter.

There are 5 types of bones in the body :
- Long bones are bones of the limbs, fingers and toes. They have lesser amounts of marrow and are made up of compact bone.
- Short bones are slightly square shaped. Bones of the wrist and ankle are short bones.
- Sesamoid bones are bones embedded in tendons that hold the tendon further away from the joint allowing increased leverage of the muscle connected.
- Irregular bones are the bones of the Spine, pelvis, and some bones of the skull. They consist of thin

layers of compact bone surrounding a spongy interior.
- Flat bones are thin, curved bones that have two parallel layers of compact bones with layer of spongy bone wedged in between them.

There are 14 bones in the face, 23 bones in each foot including the ankle, and 8 bones in each wrist. Some of the minerals present in bones are potassium, calcium, manganese, zink, and iron. The most common injury for the bone is called a fracture, where a break in the bone has occurred.

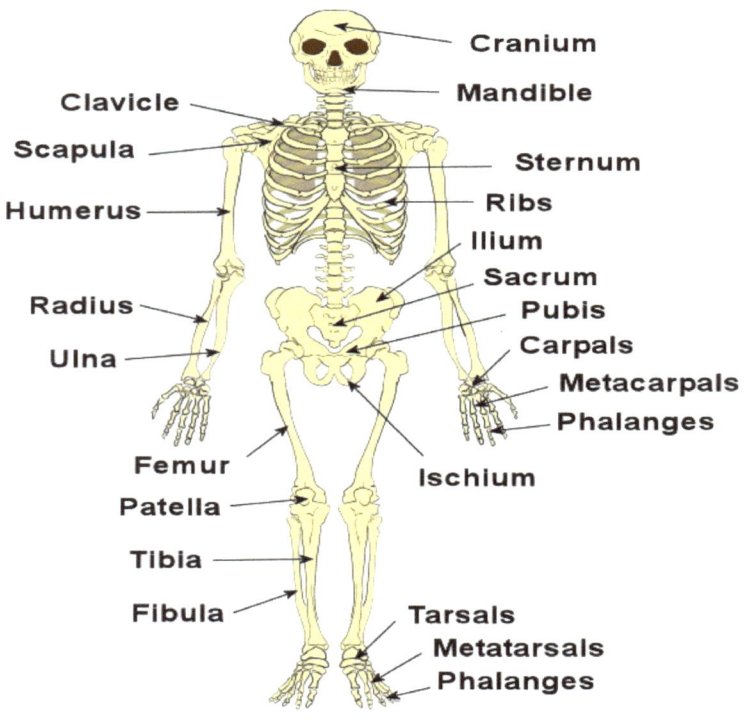

Risks
osteoporosis
arthritis
fracture
+ More

Requirements

Nutrition- Joints,bones and muscles require a great deal of nutrients. Calcium in bones is regulated, stored and removed from the bloodstream. Vitamin D helps the bones absorb calcium. It is of course better for bones to be strong rather than weak because weaker bones have a high chance of fracturing. A healthy intake of nutrients like potassium and vitamin K also will promote healthier bones.
Exercise- Exercises that force you to work against gravity help strengthen bones. Running, Dancing, Walking and some weight lifting are just a few of these healthy exercises.
Quit Smoking- smoking decreases bone mass and prevents essential absorption of calcium.

      Bones very often go through a process of breaking down and rebuilding themselves in small unnoticeable amounts. Your bones reach their peak in adults around age 30. Calcium and collagen are what make them hard. If we apply the function of the bones in the human body to life we'd have to take notice of a few things. As a whole, we can consider the skeleton to be somewhat like a frame.

Not only in the way in which a hanger supports a t-shirt, but also in the way bones limit movement to benefit various muscle groups. The service of protection provided by the bones also can be seen as a useful way to conduct our lives as well. Taking the Bone approach in life would be protecting the most important things at all costs and supporting the surrounding faculties of symbiotic relation. Lets take a business for example: The most important thing in a business is the business's ability to continue to function as a business. Therefore, the Name, the Ideas, the research, and overall heart of the business must be protected. For this reason smart business owners patent,copyright and secure these things to ensure the safety of the business and themselves. Employees from HR to crew members help the business to function in sales, recruitment, customer service, and maintenance. They can be viewed as the muscle attached to the bone; the bone in this case would be the contract or agreement that legally allows employment.

Do you currently have a support system in your life that protects the things you deem to be most precious? Is your Joy and happiness valuable enough to be secured? You have rights and regulations as a human being. Free will is simply the ability to make a choice in a situation and should be used wisely. This authority has been since the beginning of time and is solely possible due to everyone having a unique mind. This does not exclude any of us from the rules to life and laws of existence. If a human makes the choice to attempt a dangerous life threatening stunt and doesn't harken to the voice yelling in his/her mind saying "you need a parachute!" there is a clause in the free will agreement that puts that person at fault. One can then conclude that the support system of life would be based on belief, wisdom,and will to live. The mistakes we make in life have no power to change our will to live. They can only make us wiser. Life is Good so naturally if you choose to be Bad to the Bone, don't forget "you need a parachute!"

All life forms rely on Oxygen for respiration

The Body has a temperature of 98.6 degrees Fahrenheit & 37 degrees Celsius.

Afterword

I hope this information has helped you.
Many people live and never understand how much authority over their own lives they have. From the brain down; our body is a vehicle of life that works hard and is controlled only by you. The purpose of life is to be the best you possible and only today matters. You tell your self what to feel and if there's any one you cant lie to its yourself. We become unattractive when we feel unattractive. We become overweight because we allow ourselves to become or remain overweight. Life is good so we should do good things, make good decisions and live good. It's actually not hard once you've made it out of the ditch you may have created by not so good decisions. Naturally you'll still have some of the same duties and pressures, and will still encounter temptations, bad experiences and losses on some levels. Only now your in a better position and state of mind to continue to gain, to persevere, and Live on.

~Beloved, I wish above all things that thou
mayest prosper and be in good health,
even as thy soul prospereth.
-3 john :2

END..

We'll pick back up on vol.2

MAY LOVE TRUTH AND PEACE ALWAYS BE WITH YOU..

www.ingramcontent.com/pod-product-compliance
Lightning Source LLC
Chambersburg PA
CBHW042333150426
43194CB00001B/42